DANGEROUS
...OR NOT?

TOADS
AND OTHER AMPHIBIANS

TRACIE SANTOS

Rourke
Educational Media

A Division of
Carson Dellosa
Education

Before Reading: *Building Background Knowledge and Vocabulary*

Building background knowledge can help children process new information and build upon what they already know. Before reading a book, it is important to tap into what children already know about the topic. This will help them develop their vocabulary and increase their reading comprehension.

Questions and Activities to Build Background Knowledge:

1. Look at the front cover of the book and read the title. What do you think this book will be about?
2. What do you already know about this topic?
3. Take a book walk and skim the pages. Look at the table of contents, photographs, captions, and bold words. Did these text features give you any information or predictions about what you will read in this book?

Vocabulary: *Vocabulary Is Key to Reading Comprehension*

Use the following directions to prompt a conversation about each word.

- Read the vocabulary words.
- What comes to mind when you see each word?
- What do you think each word means?

Vocabulary Words:
- aggressive
- amphibians
- invasive species
- juvenile
- venom
- warts

During Reading: *Reading for Meaning and Understanding*

To achieve deep comprehension of a book, children are encouraged to use close reading strategies. During reading, it is important to have children stop and make connections. These connections result in deeper analysis and understanding of a book.

 Close Reading a Text

During reading, have children stop and talk about the following:

- Any confusing parts
- Any unknown words
- Text to text, text to self, text to world connections
- The main idea in each chapter or heading

Encourage children to use context clues to determine the meaning of any unknown words. These strategies will help children learn to analyze the text more thoroughly as they read.

When you are finished reading this book, turn to the next-to-last page for **After Reading Questions** and an **Activity**.

TABLE OF CONTENTS

WHAT MAKES AN AMPHIBIAN DANGEROUS?

What do you imagine when you think of dangerous **amphibians**? You might think of sharp claws or a strong bite. The facts may surprise you.

 amphibians (am-FIB-ee-uhns): cold-blooded animals with a backbone that live in water and breathe with gills when young; as adults, they develop lungs and live on land

Some amphibians have poison or **venom**. They can hurt animals or people. Some amphibians can take over new environments. Others only seem dangerous.

 venom (VEN-uhm): poison put into a body by biting or stinging

POISON SKIN AND SPIKY RIBS

The golden frog has poison on its skin. The poison on one frog is strong enough to kill ten people. But golden frogs are only dangerous if you eat or touch them.

Dangerous Dinner

Many poison frogs eat certain insects in the wild. Chemicals in the insects give frogs their poison. If the frogs eat different food, they are not poisonous.

LOW HIGH

DANGER METER

Cane toads have poison on their skin too.
Animals can die if they eat a cane toad. The
poison can also bother a person's skin and eyes.

11

Cane toads are an **invasive species**. They eat all of the insects in an area so other animals cannot get food. They have many babies. Not many animals eat cane toads.

LOW · HIGH
DANGER METER

invasive species (in-VAY-siv SPEE-sheez): a type of living thing that is brought into an environment and takes it over, causing harm

Here Comes Trouble

In 1955, a pet dealer accidentally released about 100 cane toads in Florida. Just a few years later, the toads had become a problem.

Iberian ribbed newts can make poison on their skin. They can push their ribs through their skin when they are in danger. But they usually stay in the water and rarely attack.

LOW HIGH

DANGER METER

15

Bruno's casque-headed frogs have sharp
spikes on their head. They use them to put
strong venom into attackers. But they are not
usually **aggressive**.

 aggressive (uh-GRES-iv): ready to attack

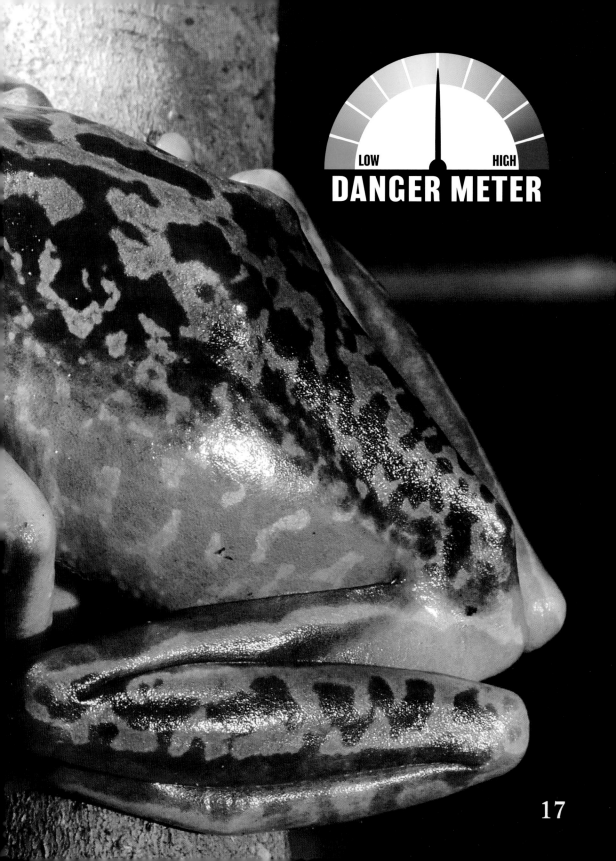

LOW HIGH

DANGER METER

17

STRANGE BUT NOT SCARY

Red efts are **juvenile** Eastern newts. Their bodies have a poison that is strongest when they are young. But they do not hurt the environment or people.

LOW   HIGH

DANGER METER

 juvenile (JOO-vuh-nuhl): in a
young stage of life

American toads have a poison that can make animals sick if eaten. The poison rarely kills animals. Some people think American toads can give you **warts** if you touch them! But this is not true.

 warts (wortz): small bumps on the skin

LOW HIGH

DANGER METER

21

Giant salamanders might look scary. But they do not attack humans. They eat snails, fish, and other water animals.

LOW HIGH
DANGER METER

Water Giants

Giant salamanders are the largest living amphibians in the world. Some can grow up to 5.9 feet (1.8 meters) long.

Caecilians look like worms with teeth. They live underground and in stream beds. They eat animals such as earthworms.

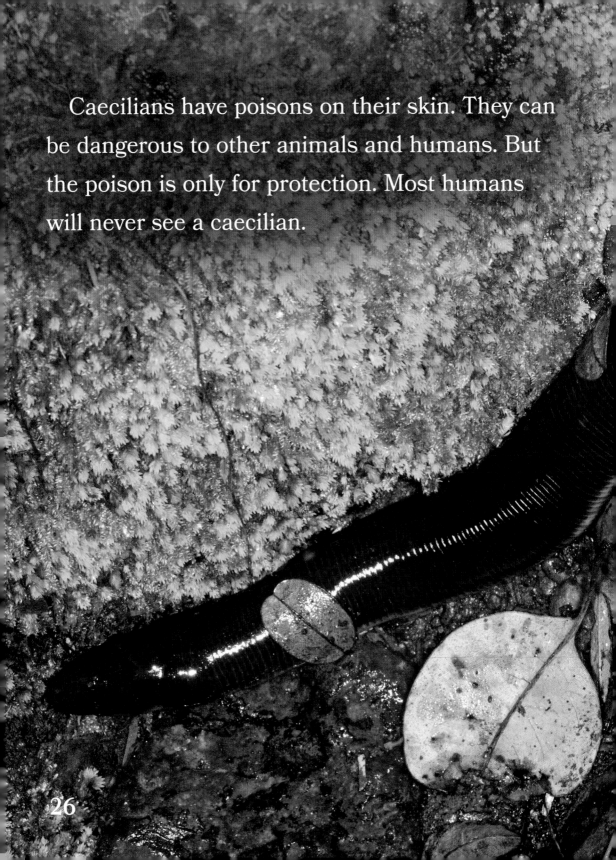

Caecilians have poisons on their skin. They can be dangerous to other animals and humans. But the poison is only for protection. Most humans will never see a caecilian.

LOW HIGH

DANGER METER

Think about the amphibians around you. How are they like the animals in this book? How are they different? What do you think: Are they dangerous...or not?

DANGER METER
LOW   HIGH
?

DANGER METER
LOW   HIGH
?

LOW HIGH

? DANGER METER

LOW HIGH

? DANGER METER

29

MEMORY GAME

Look at the pictures. What do you remember reading on the pages where each image appeared?

INDEX

AFTER READING QUESTIONS

1. What makes cane toads dangerous?
2. How do Iberian ribbed newts protect themselves?
3. What are the spikes on a Bruno's casque-headed frog for?
4. How big can giant salamanders get?
5. How do some poison frogs get their poison?

ACTIVITY

Choose your favorite amphibian from this book. How dangerous is it? Plan a museum exhibit for it. Decide which information about the amphibian you would share with the public. Write down the ways you would stay safe around it.

ABOUT THE AUTHOR

Tracie Santos loves learning and writing about animals. She has worked in zoos and aquariums with some of the world's most dangerous animals. She lives in Columbus, Ohio, with her two hairless cats, who are not dangerous but look very strange.

www.rourkeeducationalmedia.com

PHOTO CREDITS: Cover (top), page 1 (top): ©topnui7711; cover (bottom), page 1 (bottom): ©Scrograff; pages 4-5: ©JAH; pages 6-7: ©rado84; pages 8-9, 30: ©JaysonPhotography; pages 10-11, 30: ©JohnCarnemolla; pages 12-13: ©TerryJ; pages 14-15: ©JAH; pages 16-17, 30: ©Leonardo Mercon; pages 18-19, 30: ©JasonOndreicka; pages 20-21: ©SteveByland; pages 22-23, 30: ©Martin Voeller; pages 24-25, 30: ©reptiles4all; pages 26-27: ©ePhotocorp; page 28a: ©LegART; page 28b: ©Martin Voeller; page 29a: ©o2beat; page 29b: ©goldenangel; page 32: ©Taryn Lindsey

Edited by: Kim Thompson
Cover design by: Rhea Magaro-Wallace
Interior design by: Bobbie Houser

Library of Congress PCN Data

Toads and Other Amphibians / Tracie Santos
 (Dangerous...or Not?)
 ISBN 978-1-73163-824-3 (hard cover)
 ISBN 978-1-73163-901-1 (soft cover)
 ISBN 978-1-73163-978-3 (e-Book)
 ISBN 978-1-73164-055-0 (e-Pub)
Library of Congress Control Number: 2020930052

Rourke Educational Media
Printed in the United States of America
01-1942011937